Asian Cooking Made Easy: Simple Asian Recipes Without Compromising Taste

Second in a series of Asian cookbooks by Asian Cookbooks LLC

ISBN Soft cover 979-8-578182-92-1

Copyright © 2020 by Asian Cookbooks LLC

All rights reserved. No part of this book may be reproduced or transmitted in any form or by any means, electronic or mechanical, including photocopying, recording, or by any information storage and retrieval system, without permission in writing from the publisher.

Books in this Series

The Little Book of Asian Noodles: Authentic, Creative, Mouthwatering Dishes Anyone Can Make

Asian Cooking Made Easy: Simple Asian Recipes Without Compromising Taste

Asian Party Food: Tasty, Creative Asian Dishes for Any Party

To order our cookbooks, contact Asian Cookbooks LLC at asiancookbooks@yahoo.com

Asian Cooking Made Easy

Simple Asian Recipes Without Compromising Taste

by Lauren Tran

PHOTOGRAPHS BY LAUREN TRAN

To Colleen, Happy Cooking!
Lauren

ACKNOWLEDGEMENTS

Special thanks and appreciation to Pamela Taylor, Thu Ewing, Stephanie Nghiem, Denise Vivaldo, Jan Guido, and Nancy Nalley Loseke for all your love, support, encouragement, and editing of the books. This project could not have happened without you and I love you all!

ABOUT THE AUTHOR

I grew up in a large family in Viet Nam being the youngest of nine children. My parents were originally from the North, but they immigrated to the South when the country was divided into the Communist North Vietnam and the Democratic South. In 1975, South Vietnam fell to communism and my extended family of sixteen people had to escape in the middle of the night in a small fishing boat. We only had some simple pantry items on the boat and had to survive by the fish we caught. The small fishing boat was virtually on its last leg when we were rescued by a large U.S. military ship in Singapore. After a month at sea, we landed at the refugee camp at the U.S. Naval Base Subic Bay in the Philippines and later transferred to a refugee camp in Arkansas.

We needed an American sponsor to settle in the U.S. and with a family of 16 people, it was almost impossible to be able to stay together. My brothers used to work for the American Embassy in Vietnam and remembered that they had a friend named Kay McEwen who lived in Denver, Colorado but we didn't have her address. They wrote a letter to Ms. McEwen anyway asking if she could sponsor us putting just "Kay McEwen Denver, Colorado" on the envelope. An amazing miracle happened as the post office went out of their way to find her and delivered the letter for us. She was a divorced lady, so she got together with a single friend name Pat and they sponsored all sixteen of us to settle in Denver, Colorado.   My family then opened the first Vietnamese restaurant in Denver named Saigon Restaurant. We later sold that restaurant, but my siblings subsequently owned other restaurants in Colorado and Southern California. Although we are no longer in the restaurant business, my family is a family of cooks and foodies. Even in Vietnam, we were always cooking, eating, entertaining, and getting together for meals with family and friends. I remember as a child helping with the food preparations for parties including making old fashioned garnishes such as carrot flowers and apple swans.

My father was an incredibly good cook. In Vietnam, Hong Kong chefs would visit our house to teach him how to make authentic Chinese dishes such as Peking Duck. I remember him testing the recipe, making that Peking Duck over and over again. As a teenager, my father taught me knife skills and how to let my knuckles guide my knife. He would tell me that if I use my knuckles, I would never cut my fingers. Growing up during the French colonial period and educated by the French, my father also loved French culture and food. I remember him taking us to Vietnamese-French restaurants to have Lobster Thermidor and Bouillabaisse. He introduced his children to a variety of cuisines which helped me develop a palate for different tastes and flavors.

Food is definitely my passion and it is a part of who I am. Although I went on to have a Law Degree from U.S.C. Law School and practiced as a litigator in California, my love for cooking never waned and here I am back to doing what I love in writing this book.

ASIAN COOKING MADE EASY

This book contains recipes simplified by using semi-homemade shortcuts without compromising taste. It is the second cookbook in our series of Asian cookbooks. Our first in the series, The Little Book of Asian Noodles, is available on Amazon. Other upcoming cookbooks in the series include Asian Party Food and Best Asian Dishes. Every recipe is near and dear to my heart and I hope you will enjoy cooking along with me to explore the many exotic flavors of Asian cuisines!

CONTACT AND SOCIAL MEDIA

If you have questions, comments or suggestions about the ingredients or recipes, please contact me at asiancookbooks@yahoo.com.

There is a YouTube channel as a companion to the cookbooks. On there, you can find videos with instructions such as how to roll summer rolls, make fried rice, and stretch shrimp for tempura.

Instagram: instagram.com/asiancookbooks/ - @asiancookbooks

Facebook: facebook.com/asiancookbooks - @asiancookbook

YouTube: https://www.youtube.com/channel/UCEVbHgp3qOrPbJNjoSF1hOw - Asian cookbooks

Contents

ACKNOWLEDGEMENTS 4
ABOUT THE AUTHOR 5
ASIAN COOKING MADE EASY 6
CONTACT AND SOCIAL MEDIA 6
APPETIZERS, SOUPS, AND SALADS 9

    Vietnamese Summer Rolls 4 Ways – Gỏi Cuốn 10
        Grilled Beef and Shrimp Summer Rolls 10
        Salmon and Pineapple Summer Rolls 13
        Shrimp, Chicken, and Mango Summer Rolls 15
        Fruit Summer Rolls 17
    Shrimp Rocket Rolls 19
    Crispy Shrimp Cocoons 21
    Shrimp and Vegetable Tempura 22
    Bang Bang Shrimp 24
    Coconut Shrimp 25
    Lemongrass Prawns 26
    Baked Mussels with Sriracha Mayo 28
    Baked Mussels with Scallion Oil 29
    Beef and Chicken Satay Skewers 30
    Spicy Beef Lettuce Wrap 31
    Cashew Chicken Lettuce Wrap 32
    Traditional Chinese Lettuce Wrap 32
    Chicken Curry Salad Lettuce Wrap 33
    Vietnamese Mini Shrimp Pancakes – Bánh Khọt 34
    Char Siu Roast Pork Bao 36
    Roast Duck Bao 37
    Thai Hot and Sour Seafood Soup – Tom Yum 38
    Seafood Egg Drop Soup 40
    Chinese Chicken Salad 41
    Seared Tuna Salad 43
    Shrimp Mango Salad 44
    Rare Beef in Lime Juice Salad 46
    Mandarin Chicken Salad 48

ENTRÉES 51

    Cantonese-Style Ginger Scallion Lobster..52
    Singapore Crab..54
    Salt and Pepper Shrimp..55
    Black Pepper Beef..57
    Beef and Asparagus Stir-Fry..59
    Beef over French Fries..61
    Vietnamese Shaken Beef – Bò Lúc Lắc..63
    Orange Chicken..65
    Clams in Black Bean Sauce..66
    Mapo Tofu..68
    Beef Stew...70
    Chicken Curry with Coconut Cashew Rice..71
    Chicken Pineapple Fried Rice..73
    Shrimp Fried Rice...75
    Teriyaki Salmon..77
    Salmon with Crispy Rice...78
    Korean BBQ Short Ribs – Kalbi..80
    Korean BBQ Beef Tacos..81
    Miso Ramen with Chashu Pork..82
    Easy Beef Pho..85
    Instant Pot Hue-Style Spicy Beef Noodle Soup – Bún Bò Huế.....................87
    Chicken Curry Pot Pies...89
    Vietnamese Paté Chaud – Puff Pastry Meat Pies...91
    Roast Pork Bánh Mi Sandwich...93
    Steamed Shrimp with Baby Bok Choy...95
    Shitake Mushrooms with Baby Bok Choy...97

ASIAN INGREDIENT GLOSSARY 99
INDEX 107

APPETIZERS, SOUPS & SALADS

vietnamese summer rolls 4 ways – gỏi cuốn

Traditional Vietnamese summer rolls or gỏi cuốn is a refreshing Vietnamese salad roll made with rice paper consisting of cooked shrimp, pork, lettuce, cucumber, herbs, rice vermicelli, pickled carrots and daikon. The rice paper or bánh tráng is an edible wrapper made from rice starch which becomes pliable by a quick soak in water. The rice paper serves as a wrapper so the fillings can be anything you desire!

For the recipe for Vietnamese traditional summer rolls, see our first cookbook in the series, The Little Book of Asian Noodles.

Other than the traditional pork and shrimp, you can use various proteins such as beef, chicken, or salmon. You can also be creative and add fruits such as mango, pineapple, apple, or strawberries. In these non-traditional summer rolls, I eliminated the rice vermicelli and added fruits for a fun variety. The trick for tight rolls is to roll it in 2 to 3 stages. Do not put all the fillings in before rolling or the roll will be loose. Put some fillings in, roll, add more fillings, and roll. If not consumed right away, wrap tightly in plastic wrap, and do not refrigerate. If refrigerated, rice paper will be hard so rolls need to be eaten within a couple hours. They cannot be refrigerated overnight.

Create your own summer rolls for your next party or have a do it yourself party to let your guests choose their own fillings and make their own rolls. Have fun and roll away!

grilled beef and shrimp summer rolls

1 package, 25-count, 25 or 28-cm round rice paper (see ingredient glossary on page 103)

1 lb tender beef such as flank, rib eye, sliced
1 lb large shrimp, tail-on to retain shape

2 ½ Tbsp soy sauce
2 Tbsp oil
1 cup water
2 garlic cloves, chopped
5 Tbsp brown sugar
Pinch of pepper

In a large bowl, whisk together soy sauce, oil, water, garlic, brown sugar, and pepper. Divide and marinate beef and shrimp separately. Marinate beef for one hour. Grill on an outside grill or grill pan. The meat should be charred but not burned.

For shrimp, marinate for about 10 minutes and grill. Remove the tail and cut in half, lengthwise.

Cut lettuce into half, length-wise pieces, about 5-inch long. Chop mint, cilantro, and basil, or leave them whole. Cut cucumbers into long slices about 5-inch long.

Green or red leaf lettuce
Herbs – mint, cilantro, cinnamon/Thai basil (see ingredient glossary on page 100)
3 English cucumbers
Pickled carrots and daikon – see recipe below

Vietnamese dipping sauce – see recipe on page 18

Hoisin peanut sauce – see recipe on page 18

In a large bowl of warm water, soak rice paper all-around twice, making sure that water touches the whole rice paper. Don't worry that it is not fully soft yet, it will be in a few seconds. Put rice paper on a large plate, place lettuce, mint, cilantro, basil, pickled carrots/daikon, and cucumber on top, leaving spaces on the bottom and sides. Fold up from the bottom, put more cucumber on top of the rice paper just folded. Put beef and/or shrimp halves in the front with skin side down. Fold the two sides of rice paper in and roll.

Serve with Vietnamese dipping sauce or hoisin peanut sauce.

Serves 4-6

Pickled Carrots and Daikon

In a closed container or jar, add water, vinegar, sugar, salt, carrot, and daikon. Make at least one day ahead and keep refrigerated until use.

1 cup water
2 Tbsp white vinegar
2 Tbsp sugar
1 tsp salt
½ cup carrot, julienned into matchsticks strips
½ cup daikon, julienned into matchsticks strips

* See our video on YouTube on how to roll summer rolls

https://youtu.be/UzU-ienLqoo

salmon and pineapple summer rolls

1 package, 25-count, 25 or 28-cm round rice paper (see ingredient glossary on page 103)

1 lb salmon fillet
2 Tbsp oil
Pinch of salt
Pinch of pepper
2 Tbsp oyster sauce
2 Tbsp deli mustard
Pinch of garlic powder

Pineapple, cut into wedges and sliced

Green or red leaf lettuce
Herbs - mint, cilantro, cinnamon /Thai basil (see ingredient glossary on page 100)
3 English cucumbers

Vietnamese dipping sauce - see recipe on page 18

Marinate salmon with oil, salt, pepper, oyster sauce, deli mustard, and garlic powder.

Preheat oven to 450° then change to broil. Under the broiler, bake salmon for about 15 minutes or until top is lightly brown. You can also grill salmon. Cut into pieces about 1-inch wide.

Cut lettuce into half, length-wise pieces, about 5-inch long. Chop mint, cilantro, basil, or leave them whole. Cut cucumbers into long slices about 5-inch long.

In a large bowl of warm water, soak rice paper all-around twice, making sure that water touches the whole rice paper. Don't worry that it is not fully soft yet, it will be in a few seconds. Put rice paper on a large plate, place lettuce, mint, cilantro, basil, and cucumber on top, leaving spaces on the bottom and sides. Fold up from the bottom, put more cucumber and salmon on top of the rice paper just folded. Put pineapple slices in the front. Fold the two sides of rice paper in and roll.

Hoisin peanut sauce – see recipe on page 18

Serve with Vietnamese dipping sauce or hoisin peanut sauce.

Serves 4–6

* See our video on YouTube on how to roll summer rolls

https://youtu.be/UzU-ienLqoo

shrimp, chicken, and mango summer rolls

1 package, 25-count, 25 or 28-cm round rice paper (see ingredient glossary on page 103)
1 lb large shrimp, preferably shell-on or tail-on to retain shape
½ lb chicken breast

Green or red leaf lettuce
Herbs – mint, cilantro, cinnamon/Thai basil (see ingredient glossary on page 100)
2 English cucumbers
3 ripe but semi-firm mangos, cut into long slices

In a saucepan, cook chicken breast in salted water until fully cooked. Pierce the thickest part of chicken with the tip of a knife, if juices run clear and no longer pink, it is done. Let cool and slice into slices about 4-inch long.

In a saucepan, cook shrimp in salted water until pink. Let cool, remove shells, and cut in half, length-wise. Cooking shrimp with shell on keeps shrimp from curling up. If using tail-on shrimp, do not cook too long. Reserve.

Cut lettuce into half, length-wise pieces, about 5-inch long. Chop mint, cilantro, and basil, or leave them

Hoisin peanut sauce – see recipe on page 18

Vietnamese dipping sauce – see recipe on page 18

whole. Cut cucumbers into long slices about 5-inch long. In a large bowl of warm water, soak rice paper all-around twice, making sure that water touches the whole rice paper. Don't worry that it is not fully soft yet, it will be in a few seconds. Put rice paper on a large plate, place lettuce, mint, cilantro, basil, and mango on top, leaving spaces on the bottom and sides. Fold up from the bottom, put cucumber and chicken on top of the rice paper just folded. Put shrimp halves in the front with skin side down. Fold the two sides of rice paper in and roll.

Serve with hoisin peanut sauce or Vietnamese dipping sauce.

Serves 4-6

* See our video on YouTube on how to roll summer rolls

https://youtu.be/UzU-ienLqoo

fruit summer rolls

1 package, 25-count, 25 or 28-cm round rice paper (see ingredient glossary on page 103)

16-ounce spring salad mix
Herbs - mint, cilantro, chopped or leave whole
6 avocados, sliced
Nectarine, sliced
Red delicious apple, sliced
Strawberries, sliced

Sweet chili sauce (see ingredient glossary on page 104) or store-bought dressings such as honey mustard, poppy seed (I use the Briannas brand)

In a large bowl of warm water, soak rice paper all-around twice, making sure that water touches the whole rice paper. Don't worry that it is not fully soft yet, it will be in a few seconds.

Put rice paper on a large plate, place spring salad mix, mint, cilantro, avocado, and nectarine on top, leaving spaces on the bottom and sides. Fold up from the bottom, put more avocado and apple slices on top of the rice paper just folded. Put strawberries in the front. Fold the two sides of rice paper in and roll.

Serve with sweet chili sauce, or honey mustard, poppy seed dressing adding sugar to desired sweetness. For the honey mustard dressing, I added 1 tsp sugar for every tablespoon of dressing.

* See our video on YouTube on how to roll Fruit Summer Rolls but add another layer of avocado with the apple and use red delicious apple.

https://youtu.be/Uwh4PPr1l2U

Vietnamese Dipping Sauce

4 ½ Tbsp fish sauce (see ingredient glossary on page 101)
1 ¾ cups water
2 Tbsp lime juice
6 Tbsp sugar
1 large garlic clove, crushed

Optional: 1 tsp chili garlic sauce (see ingredient glossary on page 100)
Fresh chili, sliced

In a bowl, add fish sauce, water, lime juice, sugar, garlic, and stir. Let sit until sugar is dissolved or microwave for 1 minute to help it dissolve. Add chili garlic sauce and fresh chili for heat. You can also pound garlic and fresh chili in a mortar and pestle first.

This is a basic recipe only, you will have to adjust the seasoning depending on what you are serving it with such as shrimp rolls or rare beef salad. Taste it with your dish and adjust accordingly.

Hoisin Peanut Sauce

3 Tbsp hoisin sauce
2 Tbsp peanut butter
2 Tbsp oil
2 tsp sugar
¼ tsp salt
1 cup chicken broth
2 Tbsp cornstarch
¼ cup water
Chili garlic sauce (see ingredient glossary on page 100)
1/8 cup roasted peanuts, chopped

In a bowl, mix cornstarch and water to make a slurry.

In a saucepan, whisk hoisin sauce, peanut butter, oil, sugar, salt, chicken broth together and bring to a boil. Whisk in cornstarch slurry until slightly thickened and remove from heat. Add chili garlic sauce and top with chopped roasted peanuts.

shrimp rocket rolls

1 package, 50-count, 8-inch square spring roll wrappers (see ingredient glossary on page 103)

1 lb extra-large shrimp, shelled and deveined, tail-on
¼ tsp chicken seasoning powder such as Knorr
Pinch of garlic powder
¼ tsp sugar
Pinch of pepper

Sweet chili sauce for spring rolls - available at Asian markets or online (see ingredient glossary on page 104)
Vietnamese dipping sauce - see recipe on page 18

* To make spring rolls ahead of time, lightly fry spring rolls so the wrappers are firm only and keep in freezer. When ready to use, remove from freezer then fry. Do not thaw before frying.

1 Tbsp cornstarch
½ cup water

Cut spring roll wrappers into half diagonally to have 2 triangles. Keep wrappers covered while wrapping to keep from drying out.

Season shrimp with chicken seasoning powder, garlic powder, sugar, and pepper. Make halfway slanted slits ¼-inch apart across the stomach. Then using your thumb, index, and middle fingers of both hands, push down then twist your fingers to straighten the shrimp without breaking it.

Place wrapper on a large plate, place shrimp with the tail sticking out of the long side of the triangle close to the end of the wrapper. Fold wrapper on one end then when you reach close to the triangle tip, fold top over, roll some more then using glue, seal the edges at the end.

Preheat oil in deep fryer or skillet to 350° and deep fry about 5 minutes or until golden. Remove and drain on paper towel. To reheat, bake in 350° oven for 5-10 minutes until crispy. Do not refry in oil.

Serve with sweet chili sauce or Vietnamese dipping sauce.

Glue for edges

In a bowl, mix cornstarch and water, microwave for 60 seconds, or heat up in a small sauce pan until thickened and slightly translucent to use as glue for edges.

* See our video on YouTube on how to roll Shrimp Rolls

https://youtu.be/xXo2TRcMNGU

*For recipe of Vietnamese traditional spring rolls, see our first cookbook in the series, The Little Book of Asian Noodles.

crispy shrimp cocoons

14-ounce fresh egg noodles (see ingredient glossary on page 100)

1 lb extra-jumbo or colossal shrimp, shelled and deveined, leaving the tail
½ tsp salt
½ tsp pepper

Sweet chili sauce for spring rolls (see ingredient glossary on page 104)

Season shrimp with salt and pepper.

Loosen and take about 10 strands of fresh noodles, then wrap around shrimp twisting or tying the end. Preheat oil to 350° in deep fryer or skillet and deep fry about 30 seconds until golden. Remove and drain on paper towel.

Serve with sweet chili sauce.

Serves 4

shrimp and vegetable tempura

To stretch shrimp, slit halfway along the back of shrimp and devein. Then make halfway slanted slits ¼-inch apart across that slit back. Turn shrimp over and make halfway straight cut across the stomach taking care to not cut all the way. Then on the back, use your thumb, index, and middle fingers of both hands, push down then twist your fingers to flatten the shrimp without breaking it.

Cut vegetables into slices about ½-inch thick. Cut button mushrooms in half or leave whole.

In a bowl, make tempura batter according to instructions using ice water or cold club soda.

¼ lb extra large shrimp, shelled and deveined, tail-on
Vegetables such as kabocha squash, sweet potatoes, zucchini, button mushrooms
10-ounce tempura batter mix
 (see ingredient glossary on page 104)
Ice water or cold club soda
Dry flour

Preheat oil in deep fryer or skillet to 350° or drop some batter in oil and if they float to the surface, oil is hot enough. You can also put wooden chopsticks in the oil and when small bubbles formed around the chopsticks, oil is hot enough. Coat shrimp and vegetables in dry flour then dip into tempura batter and deep fry until golden. Drain on paper towel.

Serve with tempura sauce or Sriracha wasabi mayonnaise.

Serves 4-6

Tempura Sauce

1 Tbsp soy sauce
¾ cup water
3 tsp mirin

In a bowl, add soy sauce, water, and mirin.

Sriracha Wasabi Mayonnaise

¼ cup mayonnaise
¼ cup Miracle Whip
1 clove garlic, minced
½ tsp wasabi paste
1 tsp Sriracha hot chili sauce
(see ingredient glossary on page 104)
Pepper

In a bowl, mix well mayonnaise, Miracle Whip, garlic, wasabi, Sriracha, and pepper.

* See our video on YouTube on how to stretch shrimp and make tempura batter from scratch

https://youtu.be/FTcEMrSQl3I

bang bang shrimp

1 lb large shrimp, shelled and deveined
½ cup buttermilk
1 cup cornstarch
¼ cup sweet chili sauce for spring rolls (see ingredient glossary on page 104)

Preheat oil to 350° in deep fryer or skillet. Soak shrimp in buttermilk*, dredge in cornstarch, and deep fry for about 2 minutes. Remove and drain on paper towel.

In a bowl, add sweet chili sauce, mayonnaise, Sriracha hot chili sauce, and mix well.

½ cup mayonnaise
1 tsp Sriracha hot chili sauce (see ingredient glossary on page 104)

Add shrimp, toss to coat, and serve.

*You can also make buttermilk by adding ½ tablespoon white vinegar or lemon juice to enough whole milk to make ½ cup.

Serves 4-6

coconut shrimp

1 lb large shrimp, shelled and deveined, tail-on
Pinch of salt
Pinch of pepper
2 eggs
Flour
1½ cups unsweetened coconut flakes
¾ cup panko bread crumbs

Sweet chili sauce for spring rolls (see ingredient glossary on page 104)

Preheat oil in deep fryer or skillet to 350°.

Season shrimp with a sprinkle of salt and pepper.

In a bowl, beat 2 eggs. In another bowl, add flour. In a third bowl, mix unsweetened coconut flakes and panko. Dredge shrimp in eggs, flour, then coconut/panko mixture. Deep fry for about 2 minutes until lightly golden. Remove and drain on paper towel.

Serve with sweet chili sauce.

Serves 4-6

lemongrass prawns

1 lb jumbo or colossal prawns with tails, with or without shells; with or without heads
Pinch of salt
Pinch of pepper
Pinch of garlic powder
2 Tbsp butter, melted
1 tsp lime juice

4 Tbsp oil
4 Tbsp chopped lemongrass (frozen) (see ingredient glossary on page 101)

Devein prawns and slit the back as deep as possible, leaving tails. Season with salt, pepper, and garlic powder. In a bowl, add melted butter and lime juice. Drizzle butter mixture on prawns and grill on an outdoor grill or indoor grill pan. You can also bake in preheated 400° oven for 5-7 minutes. Reserve.

In a skillet, add oil, chopped lemongrass, and stir a few seconds until lightly golden but not burned. Remove from heat, add red pepper flakes and prawns. Coat

1 tsp red pepper flakes
Optional - fresh chili, sliced

prawns with lemongrass and chili slices if desired.

Serve by themselves, or with Sriracha mayo.

Serves 4-6

Sriracha Mayo

1 cup mayonnaise
2 Tbsp Sriracha hot chili sauce (see ingredient glossary on page 104)
2 cloves garlic, minced
Pepper

In a bowl, add mayonnaise, Sriracha, garlic, pepper, and mix well.

baked mussels with sriracha mayo

16 frozen green mussels

Sriracha mayo – see recipe on page 27
Lemon wedges

Soak mussels in salted water for 30 minutes to clean.

Preheat oven to 400°. Top each mussel with about 1 tablespoon Sriracha mayo, bake for 10 minutes and serve with lemon wedges.

baked mussels with scallion oil

16 frozen green mussels

¼ cup oil
5 stalks scallions, chopped

1 ½ Tbsp oyster sauce (see ingredient glossary on page 102)
1 ½ tsp lime juice
Pinch of garlic powder
Pinch of pepper

Roasted peanuts, chopped
Sriracha hot chili sauce (see ingredient glossary on page 104)
Lemon wedges

Soak mussels in salted water for 30 minutes to clean.

Preheat oven to 400°

In a skillet, add oil, scallions, and sauté until softened. Remove and reserve.

In a bowl, add oyster sauce, lime juice, garlic powder, pepper, and mix well. Top each mussel with about ¼ teaspoon sauce and bake 10 minutes.

Top with scallion oil, chopped roasted peanuts, Sriracha hot chili sauce, and serve with lemon wedges.

Serves 4

beef and chicken satay skewers

½ lb tender beef such as rib eye, flank, sliced
½ lb chicken thigh or breast, sliced or cut into long strips
1 package satay seasoning mix (see ingredient glossary on page 103)
¾ cups coconut milk
3 Tbsp oil
Cucumber salad, see recipe below

Pickled cucumber – see recipe on page 12 but use 1½ cups sliced cucumber and ½ cup sliced red onion instead of carrots and daikon

Using seasoning package A, season beef and chicken. Refrigerate for 2-3 hours. Insert in skewers and grill on an outdoor grill, charcoal grill, or an indoor grill pan.

In a saucepan, add the content of sauce mix of package B, coconut milk, and oil. Mix well and bring to a boil.

I use the Lobo brand satay seasoning mix so if you use other brands, follow the instructions for that brand.

Serve satay skewers with sauce and pickled cucumber.

Serves 4

spicy beef lettuce wrap

Iceberg, romaine, or butter lettuce
1 lb ground beef
Pinch of salt
Pinch of pepper
Pinch of garlic powder
2 Tbsp oil
¾ cup onion, chopped
¾ cup bell pepper, chopped
1 Tbsp hoisin sauce
½ Tbsp soy sauce
1 Tbsp Sriracha hot chili sauce (see ingredient glossary on page 104)
½ tsp sugar
1 tsp red pepper flakes
Fresh chili, sliced

In a skillet, add oil, onion, bell pepper, and a pinch of salt. Sauté until pepper is tender. Remove and reserve.

Add ground beef, salt, pepper, garlic powder, and using a wooden spoon to break up beef, sauté until cooked. Add onion, bell pepper, hoisin sauce, soy sauce, Sriracha hot chili sauce, sugar, red pepper flakes, and sauté until beef is slightly brown and crispy, but not overly dry. Add fresh chili for extra heat and adjust seasoning according to taste.

Serve in lettuce cup with hoisin chili sauce (see recipe on page 32).

Serves 4

cashew chicken lettuce wrap

Iceberg, romaine, or butter lettuce
1 lb ground chicken
¾ cup onion, chopped
Pinch of salt
Pinch of pepper
Pinch of garlic powder
¾ cup carrot, cut into small cubes
¾ cup celery, chopped
1 Tbsp hoisin sauce
½ Tbsp soy sauce
1 Tbsp Sriracha hot chili sauce (see ingredient glossary on page 104)
½ tsp sugar
¾ cup roasted cashew, lightly crushed

In a small saucepan, cook carrot, celery in salted water until carrot is tender but still has a bite to them (about 3-4 minutes). Remove and reserve.

In a skillet, add ground chicken, onion, salt, pepper, garlic powder, and using a wooden spoon to break up meat, sauté until cooked. Add carrot, celery, hoisin sauce, soy sauce, Sriracha hot chili sauce, sugar, and sauté until chicken is slightly brown and crispy, but not overly dry. Top with roasted cashew and adjust seasoning according to taste.

Serve in lettuce cups with hoisin chili sauce (see recipe below).

Serves 4

traditional chinese lettuce wrap

Iceberg, romaine, or butter lettuce
1 lb ground pork or chicken
¾ cup onion, chopped
Pinch of salt
Pinch of pepper
Pinch of garlic powder
¾ cup canned water chestnut, drained and chopped
1 Tbsp hoisin sauce
½ Tbsp soy sauce
1 Tbsp Sriracha hot chili sauce (see ingredient glossary on page 104)
½ tsp sugar

In a skillet, add ground meat, onion, salt, pepper, garlic powder, and using a wooden spoon to break up meat, sauté until cooked.

Add water chestnut, hoisin sauce, soy sauce, Sriracha hot chili sauce, sugar, and sauté until meat is slightly brown and crispy, but not overly dry. Adjust seasoning according to taste.

Serve in lettuce cups with hoisin chili sauce (see recipe below).

Serves 4

Hoisin Chili Sauce

½ cup hoisin sauce
4 tsp chili garlic sauce (see ingredient glossary on page 100)
4 tsp sugar

In a bowl, add hoisin sauce, chili garlic sauce, sugar, and mix well. Let sit until sugar dissolved.

chicken curry salad lettuce wrap

2 chicken breasts
3 hard boiled eggs, chopped
1¼ cups mayonnaise
2 tsp curry powder
2 scallions, chopped
1 cup celery, chopped
¼ tsp salt
Pepper
Romaine, butter, or iceberg lettuce
½ cup toasted slivered almond

In a saucepan, cook chicken breasts in salted water until done. Pierce the thickest part of chicken with the tip of a knife, if juices run clear and no longer pink, it is done. Let cool and cut into small bite-size cubes.

In a skillet, add raw slivered almond and keep stirring over medium heat until lightly brown. You can also roast in 350 degrees oven for 6 minutes, stirring after 4 minutes for even baking.

In a large bowl, add chicken, eggs, mayonnaise, curry powder, scallions, celery, salt, pepper to taste, and mix well. Refrigerate for about 30 minutes.

Spoon chicken salad into lettuce, top with toasted slivered almond, and serve.

Serves 4.

vietnamese mini shrimp pancakes - bánh khọt

24 oz frozen cooked medium shrimp (41/60), with or without tails
1 bag mini pancake mix - bột bánh khọt (see ingredient glossary on page 104)
4 cups water
1 cup coconut milk
1 tsp turmeric powder
4 scallions, chopped

Thaw cooked shrimp and sprinkle lightly with salt. Reserve.

In a large bowl, add mini pancake mix, water, coconut milk, turmeric powder, scallions, and mix well. This recipe is for the Pyramid brand flour mix which and I added turmeric powder for color. If you use other brands, follow the instructions for that brand.

Mini pancakes pan with lid
Pan spray
Lettuce – red or green leaf, butter lettuce
Mint
Cilantro
Cucumber, sliced

Vietnamese dipping sauce – see recipe on page 18
Optional – shredded carrot

On the stove, spray mini pancake pan. Add batter to about 2/3 and add shrimp. Cover with lid and cook for about 5 minutes over medium high heat until bottom is slightly dry. Remove from pan.

The mini pancakes pans sold in the U.S. do not have lids so just use any pot lid that fits.

Wrap pancakes with lettuce, mint, cilantro, cucumber, and dip in dipping sauce. Add shredded carrot to dipping sauce if desired.

Serves 6

char siu roast pork bao

12 frozen steamed bao buns, thawed (see ingredient glossary on page 104)

1 lb pork shoulder or butt
1 package roast pork seasoning mix (see ingredient glossary on page 103)
2 garlic cloves, chopped
1 Tbsp sherry cooking wine
2 tsp soy sauce

Sriracha mayo - see recipe on page 27
1 English cucumber, cut into slices about 2-inch long
Cilantro

In a bowl, rub pork liberally with roast pork seasoning mix, add garlic, cooking wine, and soy sauce. In a zip lock bag, marinate pork at least 1 hour or overnight. Turning over a couple times.

Preheat oven to 350°. Bake for 30 minutes with a tray of water bath in the lower rack to keep it from becoming dry. Turn pork over and bake another 30 minutes. Turn pork over again and increase temperature to 425° then bake another 15–20 minutes until you get some char on the surface, and pork is tender. Gauge the tenderness by piercing the meat with the tip of a knife. Let cool and slice.

In a steamer, steam bao buns a few minutes. Spread Sriracha mayo on steamed bao, add roast pork, cucumber, cilantro and serve.

*For recipe of Char Siu Roast Pork made from scratch, see our first cookbook in the series, The Little Book of Asian Noodles

Serves 4

roast duck bao

12 frozen steamed bao buns, thawed (see ingredient glossary on page 104)

4 duck legs
1 package roast duck seasoning mix (see ingredient glossary on page 103)

Hoisin sauce
Scallions, cut into thin, long strips

Soak duck in salted water about 1 hour to clean. Rinse and shake off access water.

Rub liberally with roast duck seasoning mix. Refrigerate, uncovered, overnight to dry out skin.

Preheat oven to 375°. Bake 30 minutes with skin side up. Let cool and slice.

In a steamer, steam bao buns for a few minutes. Spread hoisin sauce on steamed bao, add roast duck, scallions, and serve.

Serves 4

Shortcut tip – Char siu roast pork and roast duck can also be purchased at Chinese BBQ shops. Tell them not to cut the duck. Slice it yourself.

thai hot and sour seafood soup tom yum

¾ lbs large shrimp
6–8 mussels
3 cups chicken broth
3 cups water
2 ½ Tbsp tom yum paste (see ingredient glossary on page 104)
2 Tbsp fish sauce (see ingredient glossary on page 99)
2 Tbsp sugar

Soak mussels in salted water for 30 minutes to clean.

In a pot, add chicken broth, water, tom yum paste, fish sauce, sugar, onion, straw mushrooms, and simmer for 20 minutes.

Add button mushrooms, mussels, and simmer for another 5 minutes until mushroom is tender. Add shrimp and remove when turned pink. Add 2 tablespoons or more chili oil and fresh chili for extra heat. Adjust seasoning according to taste.

1 onion
1 can straw mushrooms, drained, cut in half or sliced (see ingredient glossary on page 104)
4 ounces button mushrooms, sliced

Chili oil – see recipe below

Fresh chili, sliced
Cilantro, chopped

In a soup bowl, add soup, shrimp, top with chopped cilantro, and serve with lime wedges.

Serves 2-4

Chili Oil

¼ oil
4 scallions, chopped
2 garlic cloves, chopped
2 Tbsp paprika
1 tsp red pepper flakes or more for extra heat

In a skillet, add oil, scallions, and sauté until softened. Add garlic and sauté a few seconds until garlic softened but not burned. Remove from heat, add paprika, and red pepper flakes. Reserve.

*For the recipe of Thai Tom Yum soup made from scratch, see our first cookbook in the series, The Little Book of Asian Noodles

seafood egg drop soup

1 cup imitation crab flakes
½ cup shrimp, cut into pieces
4 cups chicken broth
1 cup water
1 Tbsp soy sauce
2 eggs
1 cup peas and carrots

5 Tablespoons cornstarch
1 cup water

Salt to taste
Scallions, chopped

In a bowl, whisk the eggs. Reserve. In a bowl, mix cornstarch with 1 cup water to make a slurry. Reserve.

In a pot, add chicken broth, water, soy sauce, and bring to a boil. Whisk in eggs gently and swirl to still have strands of eggs. Add imitation crab, shrimp, peas and carrots. Bring to a boil and whisk in cornstarch slurry until slightly thickened. Add salt to taste, top with scallions and serve.

Serves 2-4

* See our video on YouTube on how to make Seafood Egg Drop soup

https://youtu.be/WCM50pDrDvM

chinese chicken salad

2 cups iceberg lettuce, chopped or chopped salad mix
½ cup mint, chopped
¼ cup scallions, chopped
1 small chicken breast
1 cup wonton skin, cut into strips
½ cup roasted or raw sesame seeds

In a pan, cook chicken in salted water until juices run clear. Pierce the thickest part of chicken with the tip of a knife, if juices run clear and no longer pink, it is done. Let cool and shred.

Preheat oil in deep fryer or skillet to 350°, deep fry wonton skin strips until golden. Remove and and drain on paper towel.

½ cup roasted peanuts, crushed

Store bought Sesame Ginger dressing (such as Litehouse brand in the produce section)

Toss lettuce or salad mix, mint, scallions, and chicken. On a plate, add salad, top with wonton strips, sesame seeds, and roasted peanuts. Serve with sesame ginger dressing.

Toasted Sesame Seeds

If using raw sesame seeds, toast over medium heat in a skillet, and keep stirring until lightly brown. You can also bake in preheated 300 degrees oven on a flat baking tray. Bake about 10 minutes until seeds are lightly browned. Shake pan after 5 minutes for even baking.

Serves 2

seared tuna salad

2 tuna steaks (6-ounce each)
2 Tbsp soy sauce
2 Tbsp sherry cooking wine or sake
2 tsp ginger, chopped
2 cloves garlic, minced
2 Tbsp olive oil
½ tsp sesame oil
1/8 cup toasted sesame seeds (see page 42)
 6-ounce spring salad mix

1 ½ Tbsp olive oil
2 tsp soy sauce
2 tsp seasoned rice vinegar
½ Tbsp sugar
1/8 cup water

Soy sauce
Wasabi paste

In a zip lock bag, add tuna steaks, soy sauce, cooking wine, ginger, garlic, olive oil, and sesame oil. Let marinate in refrigerator for at least 30 minutes.

In a grill pan or skillet, add 2 tablespoons oil and over high heat, sear until tuna is cooked about ¼-inch thickness. Flip over and sear the other side until it is cooked about ¼-inch thickness.   Remove and coat with sesame seeds. Slice about ½-inch thick.

In a bowl, mix olive oil, soy sauce, rice vinegar, sugar, and water, let sit until sugar dissolved or microwave for 15 seconds for sugar to dissolve for dressing.

On a plate, add spring salad mix, drizzle with dressing, top with tuna, and serve with wasabi soy dipping sauce.

Serves 2

shrimp mango salad

6-8 large shrimps, shelled and deveined, with or without tails
½ Tbsp oil
¼ tsp salt
¼ tsp pepper
¼ tsp garlic powder
1 tsp lime juice

4 cups cabbage or coleslaw mix
1 cup onion, very thinly sliced
2 cups semi-ripe mango
2 cups cucumber
½ cup mint, chopped
½ cup cilantro, chopped
½ cup roasted peanuts, chopped
Store bought Honey Mustard or homemade Asian Lime Dressing – see recipe below

Season shrimp with oil, salt, pepper, garlic powder, lime juice, and grill or sauté until pink. Reserve.

Cut cabbage into thin, long strips or shred. Cut mango and cucumber into long, matchstick strips

In a bowl, add cabbage or coleslaw mix, onion, mango, cucumber, mint, cilantro, dressing, and toss. On a platter, add salad and shrimp. Top with chopped roasted peanuts and serve.

Serves 4

Asian Lime Dressing

2 Tbsp oil
2 Tbsp fish sauce (see ingredient glossary on page 101) or 1 tsp salt
2 Tbsp lime juice
¼ cup water
¼ cup sugar
Pinch of pepper

In a bowl, closed container or jar, add oil, fish sauce or salt, lime juice, water, sugar, and pepper. Whisk or shake to mix well. You can also microwave for 1 minute to help sugar dissolve. Adjust seasoning according to taste.

rare beef in lime juice salad

½ lb eye of round or tenderloin, very thinly sliced
¼ cup lime juice
2 tsp fish sauce chopped (see ingredient glossary on page 101)
2 tsp sugar

2 cups cabbage, shredded or coleslaw mix
½ cup mint, chopped
½ cup Vietnamese coriander - rau ram, chopped (see ingredient glossary on page 104)
1 cup red onion, sliced
½ cup shallots, fresh, dried, or fried
1 cup roasted peanuts, chopped
Fresh chili, sliced

Vietnamese dipping sauce - see recipe on page 18

Put beef eye of round or tenderloin in freezer until semi-frozen, then using an ultra-sharp knife, slice very thinly. Many Asian markets sell raw beef eye of round already thinly sliced for rare beef pho. It can be used for this salad as well.

In a skillet, add 1 tablespoon oil, shallots, then fry until crispy. If using dried shallots, fry and remove from heat as soon as they are golden. Dried shallots will continue to fry in hot oil and burn easily so remove heat right away when crispy but not burned. Remove and reserve. You can also purchase fried shallots at Asian markets or online.

In a bowl, add beef, lime juice, fish sauce, and sugar. Let sit until beef is slightly cooked by lime juice (about 5-10 minutes). Alternatively, quickly sauté beef in a skillet before adding to lime juice mix.

On a large plate, toss cabbage or coleslaw mix, mint, Vietnamese coriander, and drizzle with dipping sauce. Top with beef, red onion, crispy shallots, chopped roasted peanuts, and fresh chili for heat. Serve with extra dipping sauce on the side.

Serves 2-4

mandarin chicken salad

5-ounce spring mix salad

1 small chicken breast
1 Tbsp oil
1 Tbsp oyster sauce (see ingredient glossary on page 102)
1 Tbsp brown mustard
Pinch of garlic powder
Pinch of salt
Pinch of pepper
¼ cup white wine

1 small can (11-ounce) mandarin oranges, drained, reserve syrup for homemade dressing

Marinate chicken breast with oil, oyster sauce, brown mustard, garlic powder, salt, and pepper for 30 minutes.

Preheat oven to 350°. Line baking pan with foil for easy cleaning and add chicken. Pour wine in the pan, **around** the chicken but not on it, so it won't wash away the marinade. The wine evaporates and helps keep chicken breast moist during baking while adding flavor. Bake for about 30 minutes. Pierce the thickest part of chicken with the tip of a knife, if juices run clear and no longer pink, it is done. Let cool and slice.

In a skillet, add raw sliced almond and keep stirring over medium heat until lightly brown. You can also roast in 300° oven for 8 minutes, stirring after 4 minutes for even baking.

1 cup tomatoes, chopped
3 hard boiled eggs sliced or cut into wedges
2 avocados, sliced
½ cup sliced almond

Store bought honey mustard dressing (Briannas brand recommended) or homemade – see recipe below

1 Tbsp oil
2 Tbsp canned mandarin orange syrup
1 Tbsp honey
1 tsp brown mustard
½ tsp salt

In a platter or salad bowl, add spring salad mix, chicken, mandarin oranges, tomatoes, hard-boiled eggs, avocado, and toasted sliced almond. Serve with honey mustard dressing.

Honey Mustard Dressing

In a bowl, closed container or jar, add oil, mandarin orange syrup, honey, mustard, and salt. Whisk or shake to mix well.

Serves 2

ENTRÉES

cantonese-style ginger scallion lobster

If using live lobster, put lobster in freezer for 15 minutes. Either plunge a knife into lobster carapace (part of exoskeleton on the back) or blanch in boiling water, plunging headfirst, for about 2 minutes.

Remove head, cut or twist off claws, and cut off smaller legs. Remove inedible parts. Rinse lobster clean.

Split lobster tail in half lengthwise, cut into large pieces at the joints retaining shells. Separate claws at the elbow joints and crush, using a cleaver or metal meat

2 lbs live lobster or raw lobster tails
2 Tbsp cornstarch
4 Tbsp flour
4 slices ginger (1/8-inch thick), cut into matchstick strips
3 scallions, cut into 2-inch pieces
¼ cup Shaoxing or sherry cooking wine

¼ cup chicken broth
2 Tbsp cornstarch

½ Tbsp soy sauce
¼ tsp sesame oil
Pepper

Oil to fry

tenderizer, remove the shell of the big claws except for its little claw. Pat dry with paper towel. In a small bowl, mix 2 tablespoons cornstarch and 4 tablespoons flour.

In a large bowl, add lobster and sprinkle flour mix on lobster then shake bowl to coat.

Preheat oil in deep fryer or skillet to 350°. Shake off excess flour and deep fry lobster for about 15 seconds. Remove and drain on paper towel.

In a bowl, add chicken broth, cornstarch, soy sauce, sesame oil, pepper, and mix well. This is your stir-fry sauce.

In a wok or skillet, add 2 tablespoons oil, ginger, and sauté until fragrant but not burned. Over high heat, add lobster, white parts of scallions, and sauté for about 30 seconds. Add cooking wine and cover. Cook for about 2 minutes.

Add stir-fry sauce and green parts of scallions. Toss through until sauce evaporated and coats lobster then serve.

Serves 2

singapore crab

1 Dungeness crab (2-3 lbs)
¼ cup white wine
2 cups water
8-ounce can tomato sauce
2 Tbsp crab with soya bean oil (see ingredient glossary on pag 100)
1 Tbsp sugar
1 Tbsp chili garlic sauce (see ingredient glossary on page 100)
Fresh chili, sliced
½ tsp salt
1 egg, beaten
8 frozen steamed bao buns, thawed (see ingredient glossary on page 104).
Lime or lemon wedges
Scallion, chopped
Cilantro, chopped

Fill pot halfway with water, add crab and wine. Cook cover 15 minutes. Remove and let cool. Discard inedible parts and keep the top shell as well as the brain. Cut body into large pieces, and crack the claws.

In a large pot, add crab, 2 cups water, tomato sauce, crab with soya bean oil, sugar, chili garlic sauce, fresh chili, and salt. Cook cover for 5 minutes and remove crab to a serving plate.

Bring sauce to a boil, add egg, and whisk. Pour sauce over crab, top with chopped scallions and cilantro.

In a steamer, steam bao buns for a few minutes. Serve with steamed bao and lime/lemon wedges.

Serves 2

salt and pepper shrimp

1 lb large shrimp, with shells, with or without heads
6 large garlic cloves, finely chopped
3 scallions, chopped
1 Tbsp salt
1 tsp pepper
Jalapeno, sliced
1 cup flour or cornstarch

Clean and devein shrimp with a round toothpick, leaving shell.

In a skillet or wok, add 2 tablespoons oil, chopped garlic, and sauté until lightly brown but not burned. Remove and reserve.

Add another 2 tablespoons oil, scallions, and sauté until softened. Remove heat, add garlic back in (reserving some for garnishing), salt, pepper, jalapeno, and mix through. Remove and reserve.

In a large bowl, add shrimp and flour or cornstarch. Toss through to coat shrimp.

Preheat oil to 350° in deep fryer or skillet. Deep fry shrimp 1-2 minutes. Remove and add to garlic/scallions mixture right away. Toss through.

Garnish with the rest of crispy garlic and serve with rice or alone as beer food.

Serves 4

*See our video on YouTube on how to make Salt and Pepper Shrimp

https://youtu.be/yD4hJFnTXcU

* See our video on YouTube on how to devein shrimp without removing shell

https://youtu.be/Mz5N_YQZQVY

black pepper beef

½ lb tender beef such as rib eye, flank, tenderloin, sliced
Optional: ½ tsp baking soda

1 clove garlic, chopped
1/8 tsp salt
1 tsp coarsely grounded pepper
½ Tbsp soy sauce
½ Tbsp oyster sauce (see ingredient glossary on page 102)

Optional: If using a tough cut of beef, add ½ tsp baking soda to beef and let sit 20 minutes to tenderize. Rinse beef thoroughly.

In a bowl or zip lock bag, add beef, garlic, salt, pepper, soy sauce, oyster sauce, sesame oil, cornstarch, and marinate for about 30 minutes.

In a skillet, add 1 tablespoon oil, bell pepper, and saute until tender. Remove and reserve.

¼ tsp sesame oil
1 tsp cornstarch
½ red bell pepper, cut into strips
2 stalks scallions, cut into pieces about 2-inch long

Add another 2 tablespoons oil and sear beef on high heat. Do in different batches if necessary, do not overcrowd skillet.

Add bell pepper, scallions, toss through, and serve.

Serves 2

beef and asparagus stir-fry

½ lb beef such as flank, tenderloin, rib eye, bottom round, sliced
Optional: ½ tsp baking soda

2 Tbsp oil
2 cloves garlic, crushed
½ Tbsp oyster sauce (see ingredient glossary on page 102)
Black pepper

½ medium onion, sliced along the grain
Pinch of salt

1 ½ Tbsp cornstarch
¼ cup water

½ cup water
1 cup chicken broth
1 Tbsp oyster sauce
½ Tbsp soy sauce
¼ tsp sesame oil
½ lb asparagus cut into stalks about 1 ½-inch long

Scallions, chopped

Optional: If using a tough cut of beef, add ½ tsp baking soda to beef and let sit 20 minutes to tenderize. Rinse beef thoroughly before marinating.

In a bowl or zip lock bag, add beef, oil, garlic, oyster sauce, pepper, and marinate about 30 minutes.

In a small bowl, whisk cornstarch with ¼ cup water to make a slurry. Reserve.

In a wok or skillet, add 1 tablespoon oil, onion, pinch of salt, and sauté until slightly translucent. Remove and reserve.

Add another 2 tablespoons oil and over high heat, sear beef. Do in different batches if necessary, do not overcrowd skillet. Remove and reserve.

Add water, chicken broth, oyster sauce, soy sauce, sesame oil, and asparagus. Cook about 2-3 minutes until the asparagus is tender but still has a bite to them.

Add beef, onion, bring sauce to a boil. Whisk in cornstarch slurry and toss through until sauce thickened. Adjust seasoning according to taste. Top with chopped scallions and serve.

Serves 2

* See our video on YouTube on how to make Beef and Asparagus Stir-Fry

https://youtu.be/SnEMAuCTs7Y

beef over french fries

1 large McDonald's or 2 cups French fries without salt

½ lb beef such as tenderloin, rib eye, bottom round, sliced

Optional: ½ tsp baking soda

2 Tbsp oil
2 cloves garlic, crushed
½ Tbsp oyster sauce (see ingredient glossary on page 102)
Black pepper

½ medium onion, sliced along the grain
Pinch of salt

Purchase McDonald's French fries without salt. They will ask you to wait a few minutes while they make it.

Optional: If using a tough cut of beef, add ½ tsp baking soda to beef and let sit 20 minutes to tenderize. Rinse beef thoroughly before marinating.

In a bowl or zip lock bag, add beef, oil, garlic, oyster sauce, pepper, and marinate for about 30 minutes.

In a small bowl, whisk cornstarch with ¼ cup water to make a slurry. Reserve.

In a wok or skillet, add 1 tablespoon oil, onion, pinch of salt, and sauté until slightly translucent. Remove and reserve.

1 ½ Tbsp cornstarch
¼ cup water

1 cup chicken broth
½ cup water
1 Tbsp oyster sauce
1 tsp soy sauce
½ tsp sesame oil

Scallions, chopped

Add another 2 tablespoons oil and over high heat, sear beef. Do in different batches if necessary, do not overcrowd skillet.

Add onion, chicken broth, water, oyster sauce, soy sauce, sesame oil, and bring to a boil. Whisk in cornstarch slurry and toss through until sauce thickened. Adjust seasoning according to taste.

Top with scallions and serve over French fries.

Serves 2

vietnamese shaken beef
bò lúc lắc

½ lb tender beef such as rib eye or tenderloin, cut into cubes
½ Tbsp oil
1 tsp soy sauce
½ Tbsp oyster sauce (see ingredient glossary on page 102)
Pinch of pepper

½ onion, sliced along the grain

¼ cup fresh shallots, sliced, dried shallots, or fried

Chopped lettuce or watercress
2 tomatoes, sliced
¼ onion, very thinly sliced

2 Tbsp oil
2 Tbsp water
2 tsp vinegar
2 tsp sugar
½ tsp salt
Pinch of pepper

Cilantro, chopped

In a bowl or zip lock bag, add beef, oil, soy sauce, oyster sauce, pepper, and marinate for about 30 minutes.

In a wok or skillet (preferably cast iron), add 1 tablespoon oil, onion, pinch of salt, and sauté until slightly translucent. Remove and reserve.

Add another 2 tablespoons oil, and let come to searing hot. Add beef and quickly sear all sides until there are some char. Traditionally, you would shake the wok over very high heat, hence, the term "shaken" beef. Do in different batches if necessary, do not overcrowd skillet. Add onion and toss through.

In a skillet, add 1 tablespoon oil, shallots, and fry until crispy. If using dried shallots, fry and remove from heat as soon as they are golden. Dried shallots will continue to fry in hot oil and burn easily so remove from heat right away when crispy but not burned. You can also purchase fried shallots at Asian markets or online.

In a bowl, add oil, water, vinegar, sugar, salt, and pepper to make the dressing.

On a plate, add lettuce or watercress, tomatoes, thinly sliced onion, and a drizzle of dressing. Add beef, top with crispy shallots, chopped cilantro, and serve.

Serves 2

orange chicken

**4 boneless, skinless chicken thighs, cut into large bite size pieces about 1-inch
Pinch of salt
Pinch of pepper**

**2 eggs
¾ cup cornstarch
¼ cup all purpose flour**

**1 cup sweet chili sauce for spring rolls (see ingredient glossary on page 104)
¼ cup orange juice**

Season chicken pieces with salt and pepper.

In a shallow bowl, beat the eggs. In another bowl, mix cornstarch and flour.

Preheat oil in deep fryer or skillet to 350°. Dip chicken in eggs, then flour mixture, and deep fry for 5 minutes. Remove and drain on paper towel.

In a sauce pan, add sweet chili sauce, orange juice, and warm up sauce. Coat chicken pieces in sauce and serve.

Serves 2

clams in black bean sauce

2 lbs manila/steamer clams
2 Tbsp oil
3 slices ginger, ¼-inch thick, chopped
2 cups water
½ cup white wine
½ Tbsp black bean sauce (see ingredient glossary on page 100)
1 tsp sugar
1 tsp sesame oil
¼ cup cinnamon/Thai basil, roughly chopped and extra for garnishing (see ingredient glossary on page 100)

3 Tbsp cornstarch
½ cup water

2 stalks scallions, cut into 2-inch pieces
Fresh chili or jalapeño, sliced

In a small bowl, mix cornstarch and ½ cup water to make a slurry. Reserve.

In a wok or skillet, add oil, ginger, and sauté a few seconds until fragrant. Add clams, water, white wine, cover, and bring to a boil until clams open.

Add black bean sauce, sugar, sesame oil, cinnamon basil, and toss through. Whisk in cornstarch slurry until sauce thickened. Add scallions, toss through and remove from heat. Adjust seasoning according to taste.

Top with more cinnamon basil, chili slices, and serve.

Serves 2-4

68

mapo tofu

14-ounce soft/silken tofu
2 Tbsp oil
2 garlic cloves, chopped
3 slices ginger, ¼-inch thick, chopped
½ lb ground pork
2 Tbsp spicy bean sauce – Mapo sauce (see ingredient glossary on page 102)
1 tsp soy sauce
½ tsp sugar
1 cup chicken broth

3 Tbsp cornstarch
½ cup water

3 Tbsp chili oil – see recipe on page 39
Red pepper flakes
Scallions, chopped

Drain tofu and cut into small cubes. Reserve.

In a small bowl, mix cornstarch and ½ cup water to make a slurry. Reserve.

In a skillet, add oil, garlic, and ginger. Sauté a few seconds until fragrant, and add ground pork. Over high heat and using a wooden spoon, break up pork and sauté until cooked. Add spicy bean sauce, soy sauce, sugar, chicken broth, and bring to a boil. Whisk in cornstarch slurry until sauce thickened. Add tofu, chili oil, red pepper flakes to level of heat desired and toss through. Adjust seasoning according to taste.

Top with chopped scallions and serve.

Serves 2

beef stew

3 lbs beef brisket and chuck
6 cups water
3 cups carrot, cut into chunks
1 large onion, cut into large pieces
4 cloves garlic, chopped
½ cup beef stew seasoning (see ingredient glossary on page 100)
Scallions, chopped
Cilantro, chopped
Onion, very thinly sliced
Cinnamon/Thai basil (see ingredient glossary on pag 100)
2 French baguettes, toast under the broiler for about 2 minutes

In a large pot on the stove, add brisket and cover with water. Bring to a boil and blanch for 3 minutes. Remove and let cool then cut briskets into chunks. Blanching brisket first makes it easier to cut.

Cut beef chuck into chunks.

In a slow cooker, add brisket, beef chuck, water, carrot, onion, garlic, beef stew seasoning, and cook for 8 hours. I use the Quoc Viet beef stew seasoning mix so if you use other brands, adjust seasoning as necessary.

Top with scallions, cilantro, sliced onion, cinnamon basil and serve with crusty French bread

*For the recipe of Beef Stew made from scratch, see our first cookbook in the series, The Little Book of Asian Noodles.

chicken curry with coconut cashew rice

4 chicken thighs or 2 breasts, bone-in
Pinch of salt
Pinch of pepper
1 cup onion, cut into pieces
3 ½ cups chicken broth
2 cups water
2 cups coconut milk (do not use light coconut milk)
1 Tbsp curry powder
1 Tbsp fish sauce (see ingredient glossary on page 101)
2 cups carrot, cut into chunks

Chili oil - see recipe on page 39
Fresh chili, sliced

Scallions, chopped
Cilantro, chopped
Onion, thinly sliced

Debone chicken and cut into large bite size pieces. Reserve chicken bones.

In a large pot, add 1 tablespoon oil, chicken pieces, a pinch of salt, pepper, and sauté until completely cooked. Remove and reserve.

Add another tablespoon oil, onion, pinch of salt, and sauté until slightly translucent. Add chicken bones, chicken broth, water, coconut milk, curry powder, fish sauce, carrot, and simmer over medium heat for about 20 minutes until carrot is tender.

Add chicken pieces and cook for another 5 minutes. Remove heat, add 2 tablespoons or more chili oil and fresh chili for heat. Remove chicken bones.

Garnish with lots of chopped scallions, cilantro, sliced onion, and serve with coconut cashew rice.

coconut cashew rice

2 cups long grain rice
2 cups water
½ cup coconut milk
½ tsp salt
1 cup toasted cashews, lightly crushed

In an automatic rice cooker, add rice, water, coconut milk, and salt. When rice cooker switched to warm, stir to fluff up rice and keep on warm another hour.

Add toasted cashews, toss through, and serve.

Serves 4

* Tips – If you refrigerate rice overnight and it is dry the next day, sprinkle water on rice using your fingers, cover, and microwave. Rice will be moist again.

chicken pineapple fried rice

4 cups day old rice – see recipe below

½ lb chicken, cut into bite size pieces
½ Tbsp soy sauce or fish sauce (see ingredient glossary on page 101)
Pinch of pepper

1 cup chopped onions
2 cloves garlic, chopped
2 eggs
2 Tbsp soy sauce or fish sauce

Making fried rice is not as easy as it seems. Because the home stove is not as flaming hot as the commercial stove in restaurants, stirring rice too much will make it wet and clump together. To prevent this from occurring, I've found that by pressing the rice down and wait a few minutes, then flip it over and do the same again, the rice will remain separate.

In a bowl, add eggs, a pinch of salt, and whisk. In a wok or skillet, add 1 tablespoon oil, and over medium heat, make scrambled eggs. Remove and reserve.

Add another 2 tablespoons oil, chicken, ½ tablespoon fish sauce or soy sauce, pepper, and sauté until

1 cup frozen peas and carrots, rinsed and drained
1 cup fresh pineapple cut into bite size pieces about ½- inch
1 cup roasted cashews, lightly crushed
Cilantro, chopped
Oil

completely cooked. Remove and reserve.

Add another 2 tablespoons oil, onion, pinch of salt, and saute until slightly translucent. Add rice, 2 tablespoons soy or fish sauce, and mix well. Over high heat, press rice down with spatula and wait 2-3 minutes. Flip rice over, press down again, then wait another 2-3 minutes.

Add chicken, scrambled eggs, peas/carrots, pineapple, and toss through. You can also make a well in the rice and make scrambled eggs but I find it easier to make the eggs separately. Remove from heat, add toasted cashews and toss through. Adjust seasoning according to taste.

Top with chopped cilantro and serve.

Serves 4-6

Rice

2 cups long grain jasmine rice
2 ½ cups water

In an automatic rice cooker, add rice and water. When rice cooker switched to warm, stir to fluff up rice and keep on warm another 30 minutes.

Makes about 7 cups cooked rice

shrimp fried rice

3 cups day old rice - see recipe on page 74
1/3 lb shrimp
Pinch of salt
Pinch of pepper
Pinch of garlic powder
2 eggs
pinch of salt
¾ cup onion, chopped
2 cloves garlic, chopped

Making fried rice is not as easy as it seems. Because the home stove is not as flaming hot as the commercial stove in restaurants, stirring rice too much will make it wet and clump together. To prevent this from occurring, I've found that by pressing the rice down and wait a few minutes, then flip it over and do the same again, the rice will remain separate.

In a bowl, add eggs, a pinch of salt, and whisk. In a wok or skillet, add 1 tablespoon oil, and over medium heat,

2 tbsp soy sauce or fish sauce (see ingredient glossary on page 101)
¾ cup fresh bean sprouts or frozen peas and carrots (rinsed and drained)
Cilantro, chopped
Oil

make scrambled eggs. Remove and reserve.

Add another 2 tablespoons oil, shrimp, pinch of salt, pepper, garlic powder, and sauté until 80% cooked. Remove and reserve.

Add another 2 tablespoons oil, onion, pinch of salt, and saute until slightly translucent. Add rice, soy or fish sauce. Over high heat, press rice down with spatula, and wait 2-3 minutes. Flip rice over, press down again, then wait another 2-3 minutes.

Add scrambled eggs, shrimp, beansprouts or peas/carrots, and toss through. You can also make a well in the rice and make scrambled eggs but I find it easier to make the eggs separately. Adjust seasoning according to taste.

Top with chopped cilantro and serve.

Serves 4

* See our video on YouTube on how to make Shrimp Fried Rice

https://youtu.be/ETTmar4I7XA

teriyaki salmon

4 salmon steaks (4-6-ounce each)

1 cup orange juice
1 cup water
5 Tbsp soy sauce
5 Tbsp brown sugar
Pepper

2 Tbsp cornstarch
¼ cup water

Pinch of salt

2 stalks scallions, chopped

In a bowl, mix cornstarch and water to make a slurry.

In a saucepan, add orange juice, water, soy sauce, brown sugar, pepper, and bring to a boil. Whisk in cornstarch slurry until sauce is slightly thickened.

In a zip lock bag, marinate salmon with 1 cup teriyaki sauce for 1-2 hours. In a baking pan, add salmon and marinade. Sprinkle salmon with a pinch of salt.

Preheat oven to 450° then change to broil. Under the broiler, bake salmon for about 15 minutes or until top is lightly brown.

Glaze salmon with more teriyaki sauce, top with chopped scallions and serve.

salmon with crispy rice

4 salmon steaks (4-6-ounce each)
Pinch of salt
Pinch of pepper
Pinch of garlic powder
½ cup cornstarch

Preheat oil in a deep fryer or skillet to 350°.

Score salmon fillets into cubes, careful not to cut all the way. Season with salt, pepper, garlic powder, and lightly dredge in cornstarch. Shake off excess cornstarch, and deep fry about 5 minutes until slightly crispy. Remove and drain on paper towel. Serve with dipping sauce and crispy rice.

Salmon Dipping Sauce

2 Tbsp oyster sauce (see ingredient glossary on page 102)
4 tsp hoisin sauce
4 Tbsp water
1 tsp sugar
1 Tbsp oil
1 clove garlic, chopped

In a bowl, add oyster sauce, hoisin, water, sugar, oil, garlic, and mix well.

crispy rice

4 cups cooked rice – see recipe on page 74

2 Tbsp oil
4 cups cooked rice

2 Tbsp oil
1 cup chopped scallions

In an 8-inch nonstick skillet, add 2 tablespoons oil, scallions, and sauté until softened. Remove and reserve.

Add another 2 tablespoons oil and bring to heat. Add rice and press down with a spatula until rice is firmly packed. Over high heat, sear rice for about 5 minutes until bottom is crispy. Flip rice onto the plate and top with scallion oil. Rice only needs to be crispy on one side.

Serves 4

korean bbq short ribs – kalbi

3 lbs cross-cut beef short ribs
2 cup Korean BBQ marinade-Kalbi (see ingredient glossary on page 101)
Toasted sesame seeds – see page

1 cup store bought kimchi (see ingredient glossary on page 101)

Pickled cucumber – see recipe on page 12 but substitute carrots/daikon with cucumber

Cross-cut or flanken-style beef short ribs are available at Asian markets, Publix, Walmart, or you can ask your butcher to cut them for you. Add Kalbi marinade to cover ribs, and marinate for at least 2 hours or overnight. Grill on an outdoor grill, charcoal grill, or an indoor grill pan.

Sprinkle with toasted sesame seeds and serve with rice, kimchi, pickled cucumber, or any side dishes you prefer with your BBQ meat. One of my favorite way to eat Korean ribs is with angel hair pasta with pesto sauce and a side salad.

*For the recipe of Kalbi marinade made from scratch, see our first cookbook in the series, The Little Book of Asian Noodles.

korean bbq beef tacos

½ lb tender beef such as flank, ribeye, sliced
½ cup Korean BBQ marinade-Kalbi (see ingredient glossary on page 101)
Pinch of pepper
2 cups tomatoes, chopped
1 cup cilantro, chopped
½ tsp salt
Cabbage, shredded
1 cup store bought kimchi (see ingredient glossary on page 101)
3 avocados, sliced
Tortillas
½ cup sour cream
½ cup mayonnaise
1 Tbsp Sriracha hot chili sauce (see ingredient glossary on page 104)
1 Tbsp lime juice
¼ tsp salt
1/8 tsp garlic powder
1 Tbsp olive oil
4 soft tortillas

Marinate beef in Kalbi marinade and pepper for about 15 minutes. Grill on an outdoor grill, charcoal grill, or an indoor grill pan.

In a bowl, mix tomatoes, cilantro, and salt to make salsa.

Place beef in warm tortilla, top with salsa, cabbage, kimchi, avocado, and drizzle with taco sauce.

Taco Sauce

In a bowl, mix sour cream, mayonnaise, Sriracha, lime juice, salt, garlic powder, and olive oil.

*For recipes of Kalbi marinade and quick kimchi made from scratch, see our first cookbook in the series, The Little Book of Asian Noodles.

miso ramen with chashu pork

6 servings ramen or dry Chinese curly noodles

10 cups chicken broth or 5 cups dashi broth and 5 cups water
10 cups water
1 large onion
1 knob of ginger, lightly crushed
½ cup miso paste (see ingredients glossary on page 102)

½ lb baby bok choy, cut into pieces (see ingredients glossary on page 99)
2 Japanese fish cakes, sliced (available in the frozen or refrigerated section at Asian markets)
Eggs

In a pot, bring water to a boil and cook noodles according to instructions until tender. Rinse in cold water and drain in colander to dry.

If using dashi broth, make broth according to package instructions. I use the J- Basket Dashi No Moto packages and 2 bags make 5 cups dashi broth. Dashi broth is saltier than chicken broth so I add 5 more cups water. If you use other brands, adjust seasoning according to taste.

In a large pot, add chicken broth or dashi broth, water, onion, ginger, and simmer over medium-low heat for 30 minutes. Remove onion and ginger. Add miso paste to broth by pressing it through a mesh strainer with a handle, using a spoon. Adjust seasoning according to taste.

Cook baby bok choy in salted water. Soft stem baby bok choy only needs to be cooked for about 3 minutes until tender. Hard stem baby bok choy takes longer.

1 lb pork belly with skin
1 tsp salt
1 Tbsp oil
½ cup Korean BBQ marinade - Kalbi (see ingredients glossary on page 101)

Scallions, chopped
Optional - butter

Cut pork belly into 2 pieces about 2-inch wide, rub with salt. In a skillet (preferably cast iron), heat oil, and over high heat, sear pork belly, skin side first, pressing it down for even sear until skin is crispy. Turn pork over and sear the other side. The whole process takes about 10 minutes. In a zip lock bag, add pork belly, Kalbi marinade, and let marinate at least 2 hours or overnight. Turning over a couple times. In a slow cooker, add pork, marinade, and cook on high for 6-8 hours until tender. Gauge the tenderness by piercing meat with the tip of a knife. Let cool and slice.

In a pan, cover eggs with cold water, add white vinegar, and bring to a boil then cook 5-6 minutes more for soft boiled eggs. Vinegar helps soften eggshells. Remove and fill the pan with very cold or ice water. Add some vinegar to water again for easy peel. Using the side of the pan, gently break the shells a little bit all around then let eggs soak for 10 minutes until cool. Using the side of the pan, break egg a little more all-around then gently and carefully peel while keeping it submerged under water or holding it under cold water running faucet, letting the stream of water flow beneath the membrane. Cut in half and add to bowl.

Place noodles in soup bowl, top with chashu pork, bok choy, fish cakes, soft boiled egg, and fill with hot broth. You can also add a small pat of butter for richer broth. Garnish with chopped scallions.

Serves 6

*For the recipe of Miso Ramen with Cha Shu Pork made from scratch, see our first cookbook in the series, The Little Book of Asian Noodles

easy beef pho

2 lbs (2 packages) fresh or dry pho rice stick or pad Thai noodles (see ingredient glossary on page 102)

16 cups chicken broth
1 large whole onion with skin
1 large knob of ginger, unpeeled

Fresh pho rice stick noodles – In a large pot, bring water to a boil, blanch fresh rice stick noodles for about 30 seconds, and either add directly to soup bowl or rinse thoroughly in cold water and drain in colander to dry. If rinsed and drained, microwave noodles in bowl for 1 minute before adding broth.

Fresh pad Thai noodles – cook similar to fresh pho rice stick noodles but cook for about 2 minutes in boiling water.

1 pho spice mix package (see ingredient glossary on page 102)
1 ½ Tbsp fish sauce (see ingredient glossary on page 101)
1 ½ Tbsp sugar
11-ounce frozen cooked beef meatballs - bò viên (see ingredient glossary on page 99)
2 lbs beef eye of round

Scallions, chopped
Cilantro, chopped
Onions, thinly sliced
Cinnamon/Thai basil (see ingredient glossary on page 100)
Mung bean sprouts (see ingredient glossary on page 99)
Lime wedges
Sriracha hot chili sauce (see ingredients glossary on page 104)
Hoisin sauce
Jalapeños, sliced

Note: Personally, I do not like to add hoisin sauce to my pho because I think it makes the broth cloudy and changes taste. I put Sriracha and hoisin sauce in a separate small condiment dish and dip my meats in it.

Dry pho rice stick and pad Thai noodles – In a large pot, bring water to a boil and cook noodles according to instructions until tender. Rinse thoroughly in cold water and drain in colander to dry. Microwave noodles in bowl for 1 minute before adding broth.

Put onion and ginger in a grill pan, on an indoor/outdoor grill or directly on the stovetop. On high heat, roast and turn onion and ginger. Remove when onion is blackened all around, and ginger is charred. Remove skin from charred onion, leaving it whole. Using the side of a cleaver, a pestle or metal meat tenderizer, crush ginger, leaving it whole.

In a large pot, add chicken broth, onion, ginger, pho spice mix package, fish sauce, and sugar. Bring to a boil, reduce to medium-low heat, and simmer 30 minutes. Remove spice package and simmer another 30 minutes. Add frozen cooked beef meatballs the last 5 minutes. Remove and cut into half or slices. I use the Pho Hoa spice mix package, if you use other brands, adjust seasoning as necessary.

Put raw beef eye of round in freezer until semi-frozen, then using an ultra-sharp knife, slice very thinly. Many Asian markets sell raw beef eye of round already thinly sliced for rare beef pho.

Place noodles in soup bowl, top with rare beef slices, cooked beef meatballs, and fill with hot broth. Rare beef eye of round can also be blanched quickly in hot water before adding to bowl. Pho should be served very, very hot.

Garnish with chopped scallions, cilantro, and very thinly sliced onion. Serve with cinnamon/Thai basil, bean sprouts, lime wedges, Sriracha hot chili sauce, hoisin sauce, and sliced jalapeños for heat.

Serves 6

*For recipes of Beef, Chicken, and Instant Pot Beef Pho made from scratch, see our first cookbook in the series, The Little Book of Asian Noodles.

instant pot hue-style spicy beef noodle soup - bún bò huế

24-ounce rice vermicelli, large or extra-large size (see ingredient glossary on page 103)

1 ½ lbs oxtails
1 ½ lbs beef shank

In a large pot, bring water to a boil and cook vermicelli according to instructions until tender. Rinse thoroughly in cold water three times to wash off the starch and drain in colander to dry.

If using, trim any hair off pigs feet/trotters skin. Soak oxtails, beef shank, pigs feet/trotters in cold, salted water for about an hour, then scrub clean.

Optional – 1 lb pigs feet/trotters
1 large onion
9 cups water or to max line only
¼ cup bun bo hue seasoning mix (see ingredient glossary on page 100)
Optional – 2 stalks fresh lemongrass, crushed, fold into third and tie into bundle with twine (see ingredient glossary on page 101)

Chili oil – see recipe on page 39

Hue-style pork roll – Giò Huế or if not available, substitute with Giò Lụa, sliced – available at the refrigerated or freezer section at Asian markets (see ingredient glossary on page 105)

Scallions, chopped
Cilantro, chopped
Vietnamese coriander – rau ram, chopped (see ingredient glossary on page 104)
Onion, thinly sliced
Cabbage, very thinly sliced or shredded
Lime wedges
Fresh chili, sliced

In the Instant Pot, add oxtails, beef shank, pigs feet/trotters (if using), onion, water, bun bo hue seasoning mix, and lemongrass bundle (if using). Using high pressure in the pressure cooker, cook 45 minutes, sealing the steam. After 45 minutes, push cancel and let steam release naturally for 30 minutes. Release pressure manually. Remove oxtails, beef shank, pigs feet/trotters, discard onion and lemongrass. Add 2 tablespoons or more chili oil. Adjust seasoning according to taste. I use the Quoc Viet Bun Bo Hue seasoning mix, if you use other brands, adjust seasoning as necessary.

Let cool and slice beef shank. Slice pork roll.

Place rice vermicelli in soup bowl, top with beef, pork roll, oxtail, pigs feet/trotters (if using), and fill with hot broth. Garnish with chopped scallions, cilantro, Vietnamese coriander, and sliced onion. Serve with shredded cabbage, lime wedges, and fresh chili.

Serves 4

*For recipe of Bun Bo Hue made from scratch, see our first cookbook in the series, The Little Book of Asian Noodles

chicken curry pot pies

1 cup chicken breast, cut into small bite size cubes
½ cup onion, chopped
½ cup celery, chopped
1 cup frozen peas and carrots, rinsed and drained
1 can Campbell's Cream of Chicken Soup
¾ cup coconut milk
½ tsp curry powder

Optional- ½ Tbsp chili oil - see recipe on page 39

In a skillet, add 2 tablespoons oil, chicken, and sauté over medium heat until completely cooked. Remove and reserve.

Add another 2 tablespoons oil, onion, celery, and sauté until onion is slightly translucent. Add chicken, peas/carrots, cream of chicken soup, coconut milk, curry powder, and chili oil (if using). Serve in puff pastry shells.

Puff Pastry Shells

10 frozen puff pastry shells (do not thaw)
2 egg yolks
½ Tbsp water

Preheat oven to 425 degrees.

In a small bowl, beat egg yolks and water. Brush tops of puff pastry shells with egg wash and bake 15 minutes until golden.

Makes 10 pot pies.

vietnamese paté chaud puff pastry meat pies

4 frozen puff pastry sheets
(2 boxes)

1 lb ground pork
½ cup onion, chopped
1 Tbsp soy sauce
¼ tsp salt
¼ tsp sugar
¼ tsp pepper
2 cloves garlic, chopped

2 egg yolks
½ Tbsp water

Thaw puff pastry sheets for 30 minutes.

In a large bowl, add ground pork, onion, soy sauce, salt, sugar, pepper, garlic, and incorporate but don't over mix. Using your hand and about ¼ cup filling, form a small ball.

In a small bowl, whisk egg yolks and water. This is your egg wash.

Using 3-inch cookie or biscuit cutter, cut puff pastry sheets into 36 circles. Place meat filling in the middle of one pastry circle, using a pastry brush, brush egg wash around the edges. Cover the filling with another pastry circle, seal edges then make stripes around edges with a fork.

Using a 2 ¼-inch round cutter, make a small circle on top, then brush the top pastry with egg wash.

Preheat oven to 425°, bake 15 minutes until golden, and serve.

Makes 18 pies

See our video on YouTube on how to make Paté Chaud

https://youtu.be/TyIAHYc8CXc

roast pork bánh mì sandwich

2 long or 6 small French baguettes
1 cup mayonnaise
½ cup liver pate
Char siu roast pork, sliced – see recipe on page 36
Vietnamese pork roll – Giò Lụa, sliced – available in the deli or frozen sections at Asian markets (see ingredient glossary on page 105)
2 English cucumber, cut into long slices
Cilantro
Jalapeno, sliced
Pickled carrots and daikon – see recipe on page 12

Under the broiler, toast French baguettes for a few seconds.

Split bread in half, lengthwise, spread mayonnaise, liver pate on bread. Add char siu roast pork*, pork roll, cucumber, cilantro, jalapeno, pickled carrots and daikon.

Serves 6

Shortcut tip – Char siu roast pork can also be purchased at Chinese BBQ shops where you would see roast ducks hanging.

steamed shrimp with baby bok choy

½ lb jumbo (16/20) or colossal (13/15) shrimp, deveined, with tail
¼ lb baby bok choy, cut into half or sliced (see ingredient glossary on page 99)
1 Tbsp oyster sauce sliced (see ingredient glossary on page 102)
1 tsp sesame oil
Pinch of pepper
2 Tbsp Shaoxing or sherry cooking wine

Make a slit in the middle of the body of shrimp and pull tail through.

In a bowl, mix oyster sauce, sesame oil, pepper, and cooking wine.

On a plate, place baby bok choy and sauce mixture. Put plate in steamer, cover and steam 6 minutes. Add shrimp, cover, and steam another 1–2 minutes until bok choy is tender.

Serves 4

shitake mushrooms with baby bok choy

6-8 dry shitake mushrooms
3 cups water
¼ lb baby bok choy, cut into half or sliced (see ingredient glossary on page 99)
1 Tbsp oil
2 cloves garlic, chopped
½ cup chicken broth
2 Tbsp oyster sauce (see ingredient glossary on page 102)
1 Tbsp soy sauce
1 tsp sesame oil
Pinch of pepper

1 Tbsp cornstarch
¼ cup water

2 scallions, chopped

Soak shitake mushrooms in water overnight. Discard stems and leave mushrooms whole or cut into pieces. Strain mushroom soaking water through a sieve to remove any sand. **Reserve** mushroom soaking water.

In a small bowl, mix cornstarch with ¼ cup water to make a slurry. Reserve.

In a skillet, add oil, garlic, and sauté for a few seconds until garlic is fragrant. Add mushrooms, chicken broth, mushroom soaking water, oyster sauce, soy sauce, sesame oil, pepper, cover, and simmer under medium-low heat for 15 minutes. Add baby bok choy, and bring to a boil. Cook for 3 minutes or until bok choy is tender. Whisk in cornstarch slurry until sauce is slightly thickened. Top with scallions and serve.

Serves 2-4

asian ingredient glossary

I've included products and brands in this section that are my favorites which were used in the recipes in the book. It is not an endorsement.

Baby bok choy

There are 2 types of baby bok choy: 1) the light green, soft stem; and 2) the white, thick, hard stem baby bok choy. I only use the soft stem baby bok choy which is much more tender, has more flavor, and cooks much faster than the hard stem baby bok choy which is woodier in taste.

Bean sprouts *Cooked beef meatballs, with or without tendons bò viên/bò viên gân*

Frozen cooked beef meatballs are used in pho noodle soup and come with or without tendons. Gân means tendons. I prefer the meatballs with tendons because they have a crunchy texture

Beef stew seasoning mix - Bò kho

Bún bò Huê seasoning mix

Black bean sauce

Chili garlic sauce

Cinnamon/Thai basil

Crab paste with soya bean oil

Egg noodles

Fish sauce

Not all fish sauce is created equal! The taste can vary vastly between different brands so using a good fish sauce is very important in Southeast Asian cooking! Some are so bad that once you have used it, you cannot adjust the taste by simply adding water, sugar etc. The only brand of fish sauce I use is Viet Huong Three Crabs brand. It is less salty and pungent than other brands.

My second choice is Phú Quốc flying lion brand. It is a little saltier than Three Crabs brand but is mild as well. My least favorite brands are the bottle with the squid and the plastic square bottle. They are way too salty and cannot be adjusted with other ingredients. All recipes in this book were made with the Three Crabs brand so if you use other brands, you will have to adjust your seasoning accordingly. The approximate equivalent of fish sauce to salt is 1 tablespoon fish sauce equals ½ teaspoon salt.

Kimchi   *Korean BBQ marinade - Kalbi*

Lemongrass, fresh and chopped (frozen)

Mapo spicy bean sauce

Miso paste

Oyster sauce

My favorite brand of oyster sauce is the Lee Kum Kee Premium Oyster Flavored Sauce with the photo of the boy and lady on the canoe on the label. Although the Panda brand is also manufactured by Lee Kum Kee, it is a little saltier than the one with the canoe, but is excellent as well.

Pho rice stick, pad Thai noodles

Pho spice mix

Rice paper

Rice vermicelli

Roast duck seasoning mix

Roast pork seasoning mix
Char siu

Satay seasoning mix

Spring roll wrappers

My favorite brand of spring roll wrappers is the TYJ brand. It is thin, crispy, and easy to roll.

Sriracha hot chili sauce **Steamed bao buns, frozen**   **Straw mushrooms**

Sweet chili sauce for spring rolls   **Tempura batter mix**   **Tom Yum soup paste**

Vietnamese coriander Rau răm   **Vietnamese mini pancake mix - Bánh khọt**

Vietnamese pork roll, Hue-style pork roll - Giò lụa, giò Huế

INDEX

A
Asian lime dressing, 44

B
Baby bok choy, 99
Bake Mussels with Sriracha Mayo, 28
Bake Mussels with Scallion Oil, 29
Bang Bang Shrimp, 24
Bánh Khọt - Vietnamese Mini Shrimp Cakes, 34
Bánh Mì Sandwich, Roast Pork, 93
Bean sprouts, 99
Beef and Asparagus Stir-Fry, 59
Beef and Chicken Satay Skewers, 30
Beef over French Fries, 61
Beef meatballs, cooked – bò viên, 99
Beef Pho, Easy, 85
Beef Stew, 70
Beef stew seasoning mix, 100
Black bean sauce, 100
Black Pepper Beef, 57
Bò Lúc Lắc, Vietnamese Shaken Beef, 63
Bún bò Huế, Vietnamese Spicy Beef Noodle Soup, Instant Pot, 87
Bún bò Huế seasoning mix, 100

C
Cantonese-Style Ginger Scallion Lobster, 52
Cashew Chicken Lettuce Wrap, 32
Char Siu Roast Pork Bao, 36
Char siu roast pork seasoning mix, 103
Chicken Curry Salad Lettuce Wrap, 33
Chicken Curry with Coconut Cashew Rice, 71
Chicken Curry Pot Pies, 89
Chicken Pineapple Fried Rice, 73
Chili garlic sauce, 100
Chili oil, 39
Chinese Chicken Salad, 41
Cinnamon/Thai basil, 100
Clams in Black Bean Sauce, 66
Coconut Cashew Rice, 72
Coconut Shrimp, 25
Crab paste with soay bean oil, 100
Crispy Rice, 79
Crispy Shrimp Cocoons, 21

E
Easy Beef Pho, 85
Egg Drop Soup, Seafood, 40
Egg noodles, 100

F
Fish sauce, 101
Fruit Summer Rolls, 17

G
Ginger Scallion Lobster, Cantonese-Style, 52
Gỏi cuốn- Summer rolls, 10
    Fruit Summer Rolls, 17
    Grilled Beef and Shrimp Sumer Rolls, 10
    Salmon and Pineapple Sumer Rolls, 13
    Shrimp, Chicken and Mango Summer Rolls, 15
Giò lụa, giò Huế - Vietnamese pork rolls, Hue-style pork rolls, 105
Grilled Beef and Shrimp Summer Rolls, 10

H
Hoisin chili sauce, 32
Hoisin peanut sauce, 18
Honey mustard dressing, 49
Hue-Style Spicy Beef Noodle Soup - Bún Bò Huế, Instant Pot, 87

I
Instant Pot Vietnamese Spicy Beef Noodle Soup - Bún Bò Huế, 87

K
Kalbi - Korean BBQ marinade, 101
Kim chi, 101
Koren BBQ Short Ribs - Kalbi, 80
Korean BBQ Beef Tacos, 81
Korean BBQ marinade - Kalbi, 101

L
Lemongrass, fresh and chopped (frozen), 101
Lemongrass Shrimp, 26
Lettuce wraps:
    Cashew Chicken Lettuce Wraps, 32
    Chicken Curry Salad Lettuce Wrap, 33
    Spicy Beef Lettuce Wraps, 31
    Traditional Chinese Lettuce Wraps, 32

M
Mandarin Chicken Salad, 48
Mapo Tofu, 68
Mapo sauce, 102
Miso paste, 102
Miso Ramen with Chashu Pork, 82

O
Orange Chicken, 65
Oyster sauce, 102

P

Pad Thai noodles, 102
Paté Chaud – Puff Pastry Meat Pies, 91
Pho rice stick noodles, 102
Pho, Easy Beef, 85
Pho spice mix, 102
Pickled carrots and daikons, 12

R

Ramen, Miso with Chashu Pork, 82
Rare Beef in Lime Juice Salad, 46
Rice, cooking, 74
Rice, crispy, 79
Rice paper, 103
Rice stick noodles, pho, 102
Rice vermicelli, 103
Roast Duck Bao, 37
Roast duck seasoning mix, 103
Roast Pork Bánh Mì Sandwich, 93
Roast pork seasoning mix, char siu, 103

S

Salmon with Crispy Rice, 78
Salmon and Pineapple Sumer Rolls, 13
Salt and Pepper Shrimp, 55
Satay seasoning mix, 103
Seafood Egg Drop Soup, 40
Seared Tuna Salad, 43
Sesame seeds, toasted, 42
Shitake Mushroom with Baby Bok Choy, 97
Shrimp with Baby Bok Choy, Steamed, 95
Shrimp and Vegetable Tempura, 22
Shrimp, Chicken and Mango Summer Rolls, 15
Shrimp Fried Rice, 75
Shrimp Mango Salad, 44
Shrimp Rolls, 19
Singapore Crab, 54
Spicy bean sauce – Mapo sauce, 102
Spicy Beef Lettuce Wrap, 31
Spring roll wrappers, 103
Sriracha hot chili sauce, 104
Sriracha mayo, 27
Sriracha wasabi mayonnaise, 23
Steamed bao buns, frozen, 104
Steamed Bao
    Char Siu Roast Pork Bao, 36
    Roast Duck Bao. 37
Steamed Shrimp with Baby Bok Choy, 95
Straw mushrooms, 104
Sweet chili sauce for spring rolls, 104
Summer rolls– Gỏi cuốn
    Fruit Summer Rolls, 17

Grilled Beef and Shrimp Summer Rolls, 10
Salmon and Pineapple Sumer Rolls, 13
Shrimp, Chicken and Mango Summer Rolls, 15

T

Taco sauce, 81
Tempura batter mix, 104
Tempura, Shrimp and Vegetable, 22
Teriyaki Salmon, 77
Tempura sauce, 23
Thai/ Cinnamon basil, 100
Tom yum soup paste, 104
Thai Hot and Sour Seafood Soup - Tom Yum, 38
Traditional Chinese Lettuce Wrap, 32

V

Vegetable Tempura, 22
Vietnamese coriander – rau răm, 104
Vietnamese dipping sauce, 18
Vietnamese Mini Shrimp Pancakes - Bánh Khọt, 34
Vietnamese mini pancake mix, 104
Vietnamese Paté Chaud – Puff Pastry Meat Pies, 91
Vietnamese pork rolls, Hue-style pork rolls – Giò lụa, giò Huế, 105
Vietnamese Shaken Beef – Bò Lúc Lắc, 63
Vietnamese Spicy Beef Noodle Soup, Bún Bò Huế , 87

Made in the USA
Columbia, SC
27 April 2021